Introduction . . . .

Editorial

Every morning for two months, we made the trip to Sangath, the studio of the Indian architect Balkrishna Doshi. We would get out of the rickshaw at a nearby crossroads: all around us was a noisy throng of honking cars, motor scooters, and camel carts. In front of us loomed a high wall, overgrown with tropical plants. Beyond the wall were towering trees. Stepping through a gate, we entered into a wondrous garden that also housed the studio. The din of the town slowly faded away. The studio consisted of white domes, partly sunken into the ground: On hot days, staff would cool these with water flowing down in a series of cascades. Studio members would meet for the daily chai break in the shaded garden, which was also used for reviews and the model workshop. Sometimes monkeys romp on the roof, only to be driven away with long sticks.

It was only after a few weeks that we noticed that, in fact, both sides of the wall were being used. A mobile kiosk, a barber, a chai wallah, and a tailor had set up their businesses between the wall and the street. The wall was used to rig up a mirror, served as windbreak and sunshade, as boundary and backrest. We were so distracted by the strange noises and smells, the traffic and the heat that we had not noticed how variously the wall was being used. With our eyes now peeled, we wandered through the city in the subsequent weeks, collecting many new impressions.

This Reading Aid is a collection of 32 observations in Ahmedabad. We were attracted by the idiosyncrasies of India's built environment: the ingenuity of the inhabitants; the characteristics of its hot climate; the diversity of its architectural styles; and the dynamism of its public space, shaped by daily rhythms and appropriations. In this everyday reality of Ahmedabad, we found an intriguing beauty that we would like to share with the reader. We understand this book as an invitation to both observe and experience this Indian metropolis in a way that otherwise would be hidden to the casual traveller.

In Ahmedabad, we often caught things leading double lives. For example: the wall around Sangath is, in one life, a property boundary that divides the private garden from the busy street. At the same time, however, it also has a public side that opens itself up to various possibilities for informal use. In Ahmedabad, the resources and the space available are fairly restricted. Precisely because of this, purposeful structures come into being whose directness and spontaneity impressed us greatly.

Chai wallahs look for shady spots or improvise simple tent constructions to shade their customers (p. 96). Even here at these simple stands where chai is sold, we can perceive the influence of the sun on Indian spatial design. The presence of the sun allows for many functions to be moved outside. Thus, the ground floor of the National Institute of Design (p. 48) is devised as an open, shaded exterior space that is used by the students for work and exhibitions. A terraced square with trees becomes a cafeteria (p. 28). The open ground floor of the Architecture Faculty CEPT (p. 24) provides working and learning space – and is also a favorite place for the students to play cricket.

Modern houses in Ahmedabad are embedded in generous gardens. In addition to providing visual pleasure through their multitude of plant life and their beauty, the gardens help improve the indoor climate. At the Villa Sarabhai (p. 124), the swimming pool cools the house. A deep

Editorial

concrete façade protects the indoor rooms of the Villa Shodhan (p. 56) from the sun, at the same time providing a home for all sorts of plants. These brise-soleil elements were similarly used by Le Corbusier in the Mill Owners' Association Building (p. 64), and draw a cooling breeze into the building.

The exterior wall of the Jama Masjid Mosque (p. 100) is colonized with informal shops that have gradually grown together into a composite building. The wall is a "primary wall," and often the starting point for accretions and additions – like a street temple (p. 32), for example. Thus a large part of the spatial quality of Ahmedabad develops via serial production of spaces on a human scale.

The background for these small-scale structures are occasionally very large buildings such as the Central Bank (p. 76) or the Premabhai Hall (p. 88), which impose themselves strongly on their surroundings. The Indian Institute of Management (p. 36) generates very beautiful exterior spaces after the fashion of English university campuses, although completely separated from the city.

Public space in Ahmedabad, on the other hand, is influenced by the daily rhythms of its inhabitants. The old town square Manek Chowk (p. 104) is used in the morning to feed cows, during the day as a car park, in the evening as a market, and at night as sleeping quarters. Once a week, the broad river bank, which serves as a flood plain, becomes the biggest bazaar (p. 84) in the town.

Pushcarts (p. 60) serve as mobile market stands for tradesmen. In this way, temporary centers of trade can spring up in streets and squares and disappear just as quickly.

The inhabitants of Ahmedabad are extremely inventive. There are often only a few basic resources and minimal space for the realization of projects. These restrictions foster idiosyncratic solutions. How, for example, can you expand your café (p. 80) if it borders on a cemetery?

Balkrishna Doshi describes change as a basic criterion of Indian life, and this aspect is also reflected in his housing projects. He describes architecture as a continuous process that is by no means ended when the building is completed. The inhabitants modify and add extensions to their surroundings, and through this appropriation process create a new type of architecture. The user therefore plays an important role in the production of space. This can be observed, for example, in the LIC apartment blocks (p. 50), which were planned while taking future additions into account.

These were some of the observations we collected while taking strolls through Ahmedabad. In the following years, further findings were added to the collection. We used photographs and notes to record our findings, which we later translated into spatial line drawings. These drawings direct attention to the focus of our observations by fading out the background and attempting to capture each of the unique situations as precisely as possible. Objects are not shown schematically, but in their particular individuality: A bed is not simply any bed, but the particular Niwar bed found here, in Ahmedabad. It is these specific observations that, in their combination, form the basic foundation of the Ahmedabad Reading Aid.

– Niklas Fanelsa, Marius Helten, Björn Martenson, Leonard Wertgen

Editorial

The Architectural Reading Aid emerged in parallel with the International Habitat Design Workshop, a program run by Balkrishna Doshi that takes place annually for two months at the Vastu Shilpa Foundation. Students from RWTH Aachen University collaborated with other international students in a workshop. This sojourn allowed us and the other students to examine, research, and discuss Ahmedabad very intensively.

Sangath

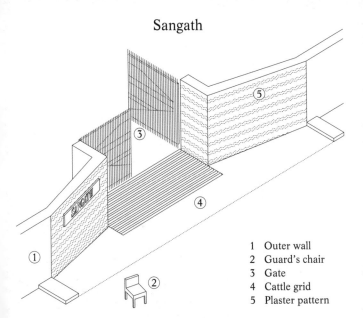

1 Outer wall
2 Guard's chair
3 Gate
4 Cattle grid
5 Plaster pattern

Balkrishna Doshi's architecture studio, named Sangath, lies on Drive In Road. The entrance is framed by a beautiful red gate standing in decorated plaster walls. A disused cattle grid on the ground tells of the agricultural fields that once surrounded the plot. Once through the gate to Sangath, the visitor finds himself in a tropical garden. Hidden speakers play Indian Folk music, blotting out the street noise. The building is a composition of different volumes, shapes, and materials. It features a series of sunken vaults and a grassy, terraced amphitheater. The main structure is set into the ground, to improve the indoor climate of the office. The roof is sheathed in a white china mosaic made from reclaimed broken crockery. On hot days, water flows over the vaulted roofs in a series of cascades.

Location: Drive In Cinema, opposite Yogi Complex, Drive In Road
Architect: Balkrishna Doshi, 1981
Program: Office of the Vastu Shilpa Foundation and
Vastu Shilpa Consultants

Sangath

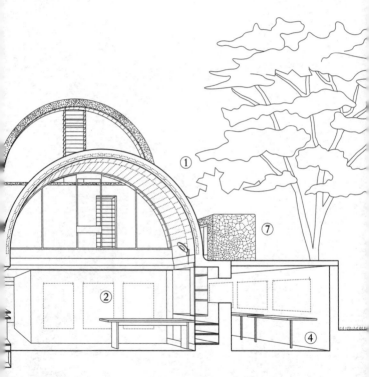

1 Vaults
2 Drawing atelier
3 Model-making workshop
4 Extension (built in 2010)
5 Outside vault

6 Water cascade
7 Skylight
8 Outer wall

1m   3m

Outer Wall

The exterior of the wall around Sangath is put to good use by various vendors. Most of the customers are passersby from the main road. Stands are set up between the road and the wall, where vendors can sit shaded by the trees in the garden. A tailor delimits his working space using old bags. For his work, he uses an iron Singer sewing machine powered with a foot pedal. The barber, on the other hand, has hung up a wooden board between the trees and the wall to serve as a canopy for his customers. He has attached a mirror and several shelves with hair products to it, as well. Spaces for seating waiting customers are shared with the chai wallah, whose improvised kitchen is composed of bricks and a huge piece of concrete guard-rail. Next to it is a large tree and the communal shrine devoted to the snake god Gogaji. On the street corner with Drive In Road stands the mobile kiosk: a former rickshaw, now repurposed by the owner to sell goods. Further down the wall are parking spaces and the entrance gate to Sangath. Sometimes, the compound's gatekeeper provides the vendors with water.

Location: Sangath, near Drive-In Cinema, opposite Yogi Complex, Drive In Road
Program: tailor, barber, chai wallah, shrine, and mobile kiosk

1 Sangath
2 Tailor
3 Barber
4 Chai wallah
5 Goga Maharaj Shrine
6 Mobile kiosk
7 "Do not hang any posters.
  Offenders will be prosecuted."
8 Sangath front gate

2m   6m

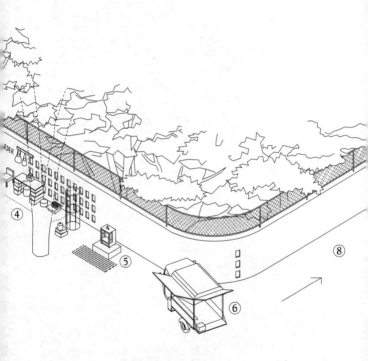

GLI Dormitory

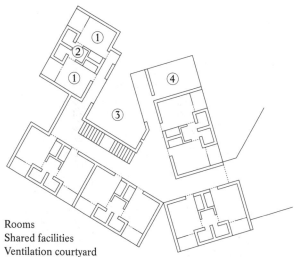

1 Rooms
2 Shared facilities
3 Ventilation courtyard
4 Common spaces

This student accommodation block is part of the Gandhi Labor Institute.
Each floor has five pairs of rooms and is centered on an internal
courtyard. The rooms here are designed as groups of two. A common
bathroom is shared by four students from two rooms. The bathroom
also serves as a connection between the rooms. Ventilation is oriented
towards the balcony, so that no ventilation window is visible on the
façade. A narrow window on the corridor allows light to fall on the desk
area. The cupboard, desk and sink are an integral part of the floor plan.

Location: Gandhi Labor Institute, Drive In Rd, Sushil Nagar Society
Architect: Balkrishna Doshi, 1984
Program: Student accommodation
Size: 40 m² per one double apartment

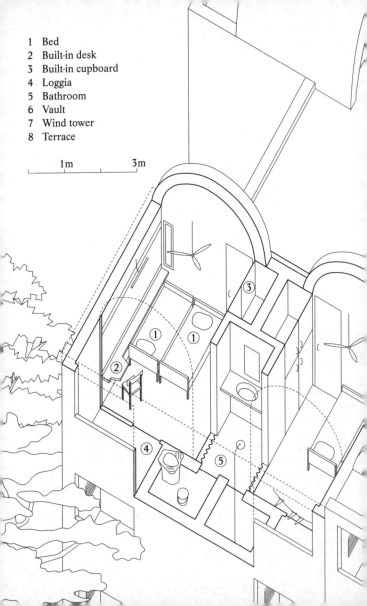

1   Bed
2   Built-in desk
3   Built-in cupboard
4   Loggia
5   Bathroom
6   Vault
7   Wind tower
8   Terrace

1m   3m

City Farm

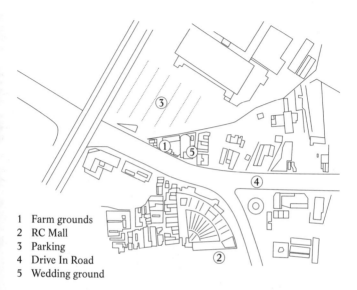

1 Farm grounds
2 RC Mall
3 Parking
4 Drive In Road
5 Wedding ground

The visitor driving down Drive In Road will notice a lot of cattle on the pavement. They belong to the City Farm, which is located next to a parking lot and opposite a large and busy shopping mall. A huge billboard provides shade for the cows. The feeding area is also equipped with fans that cool the cows while they feed. The City Farm is divided into two zones: one for feeding the animals, the second for calves. A derelict building at the front is used for hay storage. The cows are kept within the farm during the day to prevent them from causing a nuisance to traffic. The cow is believed to be a holy animal in India, so they are permitted to wander freely at night, scavenging for additional food in the rubbish heaps.

Location: Drive In Road, near Helmet Flyover, opposite R3 Mall
Program: Cattle farm, hay storage

1 Drive In Road
2 Entrance
3 Hay Storage
4 Cattle manger
5 Fan
6 Billboard
7 Area for calves

2m   6m

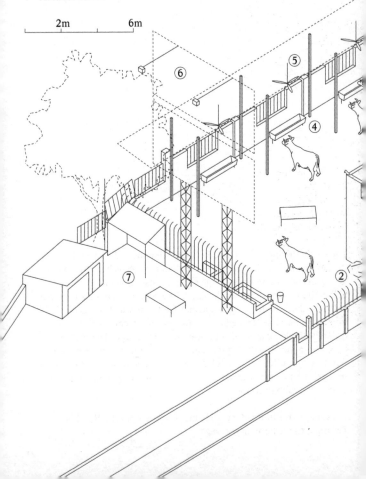

City Farm

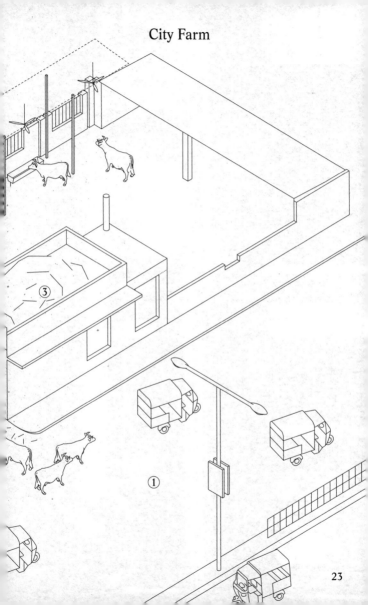

CEPT

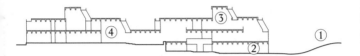

1 Lecture mounds
2 Multi-functional space
3 Studios
4 Library

The Architecture Faculty designed by Balkrishna Doshi is part of the lively tropical campus of the Centre for Environmental Planning and Technology. The building is elevated from the ground and situated in a beautiful green landscape. The Faculty's main exhibition space lies beneath the main building and is a terraced open landscape. The students use it for studying as well as for cricket and table tennis. The upper levels consist of double-height studio spaces, with north-facing windows keeping them protected from the hot sunlight from the east. Small loggias open towards the garden, where two mounds serve as an outdoor lecture theater. Doshi directed the construction of the mounds from the roof of the finished building.

Location: Center for Environmental Planning and Technology, 120 Circular Road, University Area
Architect: Balkrishna Doshi, 1968
Program: Faculty for Architecture, Cricket Pitch
Hint: The nearby Cafeteria (p. 28) serves a great lunch, which you can enjoy in the shaded seating area.

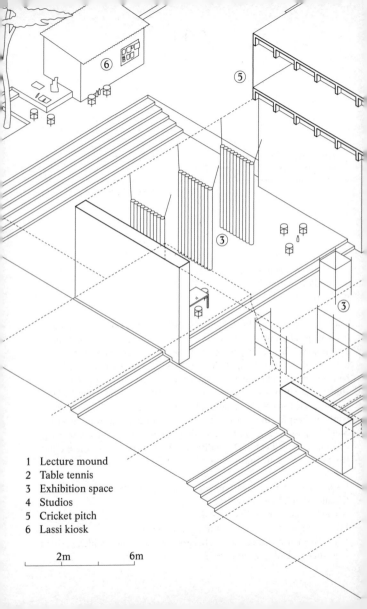

1 Lecture mound
2 Table tennis
3 Exhibition space
4 Studios
5 Cricket pitch
6 Lassi kiosk

2m   6m

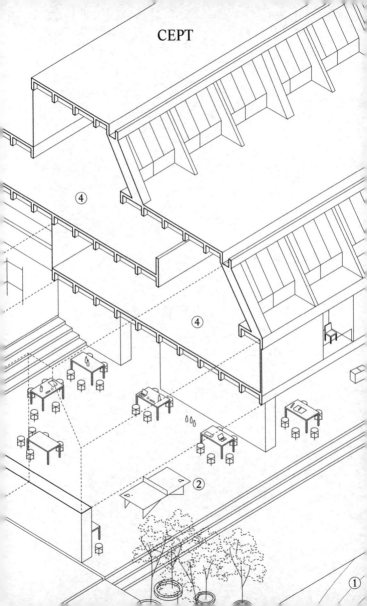

CEPT

Cafeteria

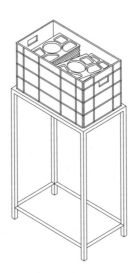

During their lunch break, many students queue up in front of the yellow door at the cafeteria. They pay for their lunch and are given a receipt to be redeemed at one of the other windows. While waiting they watch the cooks preparing their food. At the back there is an additional outside kitchen. There are lots of low walls where you can eat your lunch and chat under the leafy canopy. When you have finished the delicious lunch you put your dishes in one of the blue boxes. They stand there during opening hours and form the outside part of the cafeteria. In the evening, lamps hanging in the trees provide illumination.

Location: Behind the Center for Environment Planning and Technology, 120 Circular Road, University Area
Architect: Balkrishna Doshi, 1968
Program: Cafeteria, Seating Area
Hint: Buy meal vouchers at the counter and leave your queuing etiquette behind!

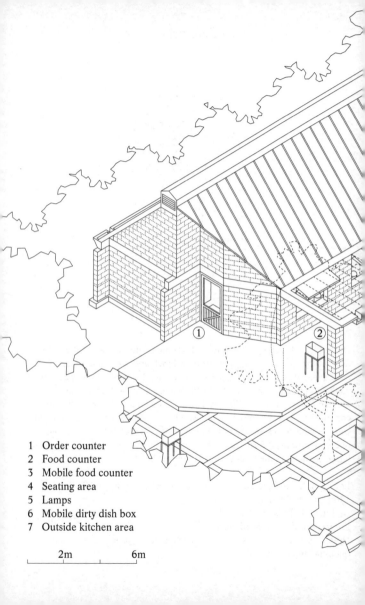

1 Order counter
2 Food counter
3 Mobile food counter
4 Seating area
5 Lamps
6 Mobile dirty dish box
7 Outside kitchen area

2m   6m

Cafeteria

31

Street Temple

Street temples of various shapes and sizes can be found on the roadsides of Ahmedabad. There is one next to the Indian Institute of Management. It is a temple to the god Shiva and is mainly visited by rickshaw drivers. It is situated on the north side of a wall and also protected from sunlight by trees and a canopy, because shade is an important factor in Hindu temples. The shrine consecrated to the relevant god is in the center of the temple. A doormat and carpet help ensure one stands before the temple with clean feet.

Location: Northern outer wall of the IIM Complex at Vikram
Sarabhai Marg, University Area
Devoted to: Shiva

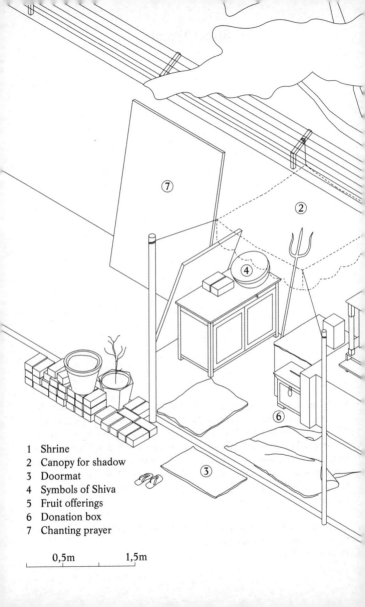

1 Shrine
2 Canopy for shadow
3 Doormat
4 Symbols of Shiva
5 Fruit offerings
6 Donation box
7 Chanting prayer

0,5m   1,5m

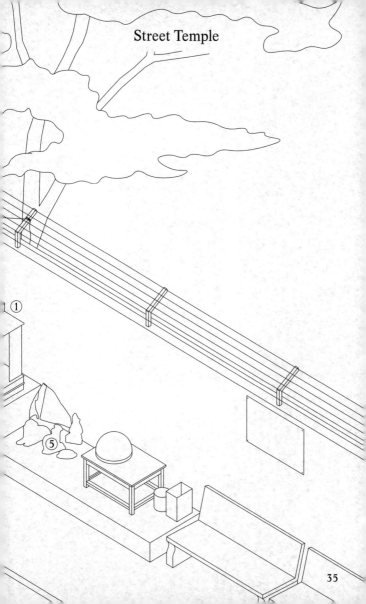

Street Temple

①

⑤

IIM

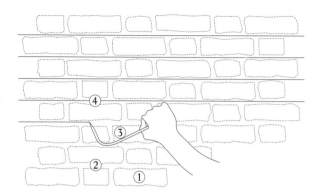

1 Bricks
2 Unfinished mortar joint
3 Tuck pointer
4 Mortar joint with even line

The IIM University Complex was designed by Louis Kahn to be like a small city with streets, houses, and squares. The impressive center court functions as a town square and is used for festive activities. Benches in the openings of the surrounding façade invite you to rest. While seated, you notice the detailing on the brick walls. There is a fine line drawn down the middle of each layer of mortar. Because the rough bricks used for the buildings's construction required thick layers of mortar, Kahn's masons began carving thin, horizontal lines into the mortar in order to give a precise character to the wall's appearance.

Location: IIM, Vastrapur, University Area
Architect: Louis I. Kahn, 1962-74
Program: Institute of Management with laboratories, library, accommodation blocks, and facilities for extracurricular activities
Size: About 28 hectares
Hint: For a guided tour, contact Mohammed Ghulam Nabi Malik (rickshaw page on the back cover)

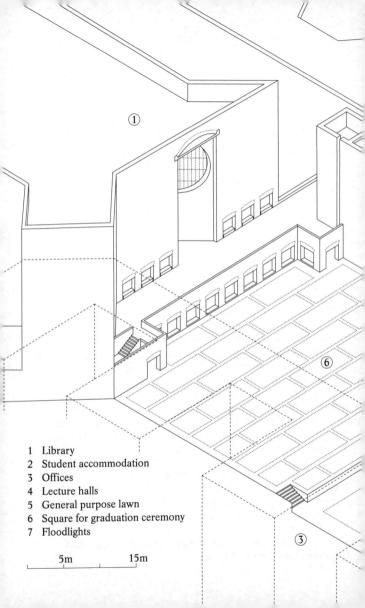

1 Library
2 Student accommodation
3 Offices
4 Lecture halls
5 General purpose lawn
6 Square for graduation ceremony
7 Floodlights

5m   15m

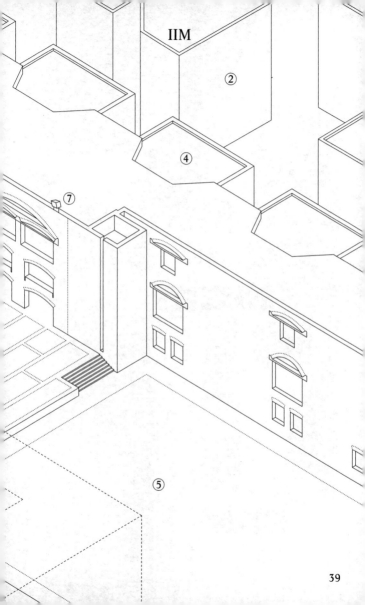

IIM

② ④ ⑦ ⑤

39

LIC Housing

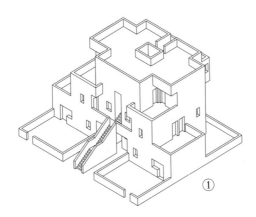

1   Without extensions

LIC Housing is a development of 54 similar houses grouped in pairs. This housing project is designed as a variation upon the traditional urban terraced house. Each block has six living units. There are three different ground plans and sizes, the biggest on the ground floor, the smallest on top, generating balconies on each level. Each apartment has the option to be extended. In time the inhabitants have adapted the houses by adding rooms, roofs and windows as a protection from the sun or the monsoon rain, creating additional living space.

Location: Life Insurance Corporation Housing Community, Bimanagar Society, near Shivranjani BRTS Bus Stop, opposite SM Road
Architect: Balkrishna Doshi, 1976
Typology: Walk-up apartment
Size: 324 housing units on 54 plots

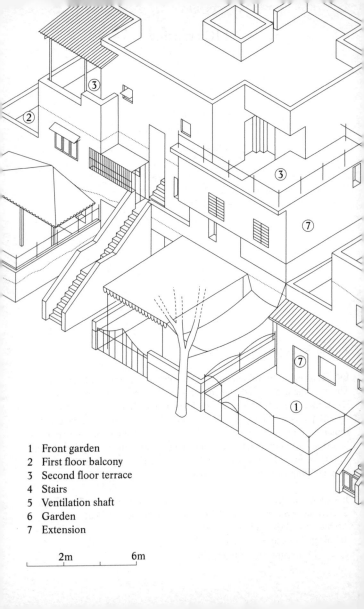

1 Front garden
2 First floor balcony
3 Second floor terrace
4 Stairs
5 Ventilation shaft
6 Garden
7 Extension

2m   6m

LIC Housing

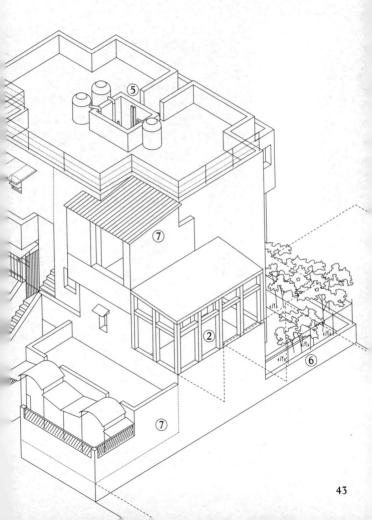

43

Sanskar Kendra

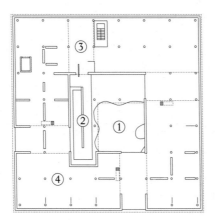

1 Courtyard
2 Ramp
3 Foyer
4 Exhibition space

The Sanskar Kendra Museum was designed by Le Corbusier as a closed box elevated from the ground. On the roof is a pool that can be filled with water on a hot day. Le Corbusier imagined a poetic experiment: flowers and plants would be put directly on the water. Then the water would be treated with fertilizer to enhance the unnatural growth of giant flowers, tomatoes and pumpkins. In the evening, visitors would wander around the artificial roof landscape. Of course none of this became reality. Nevertheless, the cool, dark exhibition spaces are worth a visit on a hot day.

Location: Opposite the National Institute of Design, Bhagtacharya Road
Architect: Le Corbusier, 1957
Program: Museum & offices, 7,500 m²

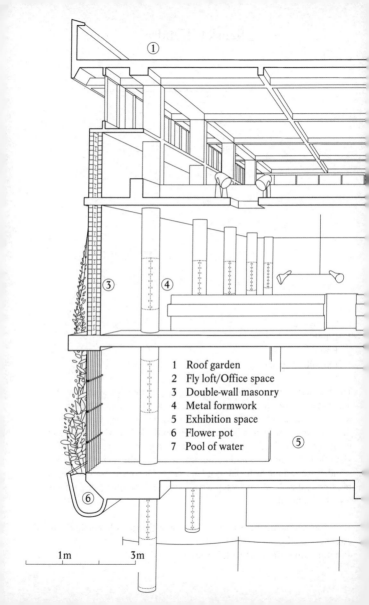

1   Roof garden
2   Fly loft/Office space
3   Double-wall masonry
4   Metal formwork
5   Exhibition space
6   Flower pot
7   Pool of water

1m   3m

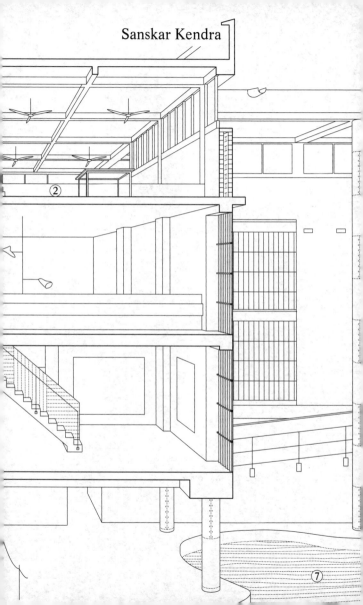

Sanskar Kendra

NID

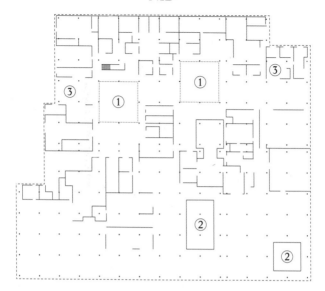

1 Inner courtyard
2 Exhibition & workspace
3 Offices

The National Institute of Design is situated on the west bank of the
Sabarmati River. The entire building rests on a floor three meters
above ground level, supported by columns. Thus the available 10,000 m²
under the building is profitably used as public space. The landscape
continues underneath the building as a furnished open space that is
used as a showroom for exhibitions and cultural events. Because the site
is flooded regularly by the nearby river, the storage spaces are located in
the upper floor.

Location: National Institute of Design, Bhagtacharya Road, Paldi
Architect: Gautam & Gira Sarabhai, Charles & Ray Eames, 1961
Program: Workshops, laboratories, drafting studios, seminar rooms,
library, offices, showrooms

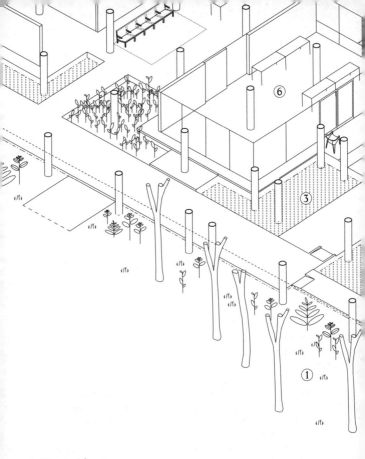

1 Tropical forest
2 Field
3 Water body
4 Exhibition space
5 Giant vases
6 Work space

2m   6m

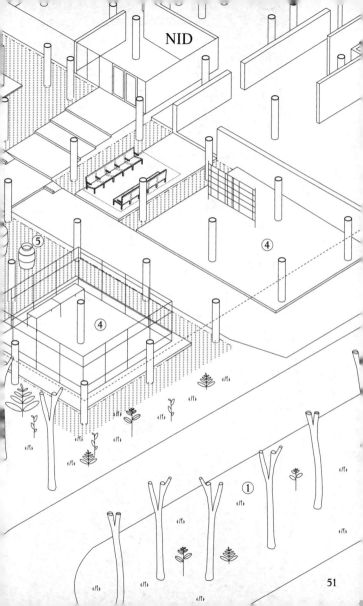

NID

⑤

④

④

①

51

Snack Cafe

The NID cafeteria is situated right next to the main building. A simple steel roof structure shades the seating area. The material is reclaimed from the roof of a nearby car park. The counter, kitchen, and seating area are situated on three terraces. Each of them is subdivided by a wide wall that serves as a bench. The chefs use the bench to prepare food, while customers use it for seating. There is no spatial separation between preparing, cooking, and eating. It all happens in one space.

Location: Behind the NID, Bhagtacharya Road, Paldi
Program: Kitchen, Cafeteria
Hint: Choose from a list of hundreds of snacks and have a cool drink from the bar.

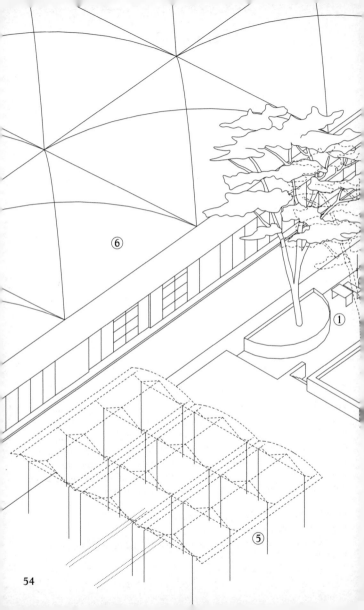

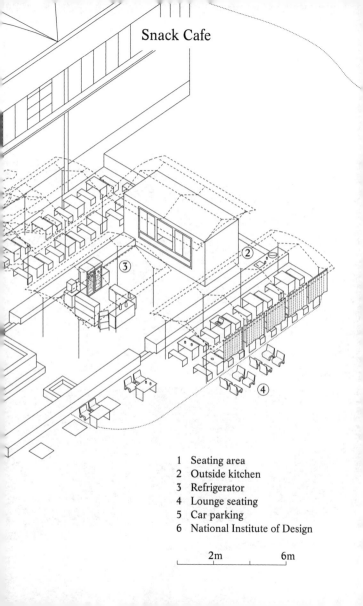

Snack Cafe

1 Seating area
2 Outside kitchen
3 Refrigerator
4 Lounge seating
5 Car parking
6 National Institute of Design

2m   6m

Villa Shodhan

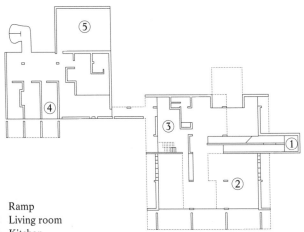

1 Ramp
2 Living room
3 Kitchen
4 Servants' quarters
5 Garage

This villa was initially designed for Surottam Hutheesing, President of the Ahmedabad Mill Owners' Association (p. 72). In the end, the luxurious bachelor residence was actually built for Shyamubhai Shodhan on an entirely different plot. A parasol roof above the whole house shelters single- and double-height spaces. The raw concrete façade is structured by brise-soleil elements. The living rooms of the villa are located behind the deep façade of sun shades. There is a large terrace with benches and plants on the parasol roof, where the owner and his guests can enjoy the view over the garden.

Location: Near Nagri Hospital, Netaji Bus stop
Architect: Le Corbusier, 1956
Hint: The building is used as a private residence and therefore is not open to visitors. You can catch glimpses of it from the nearby park.

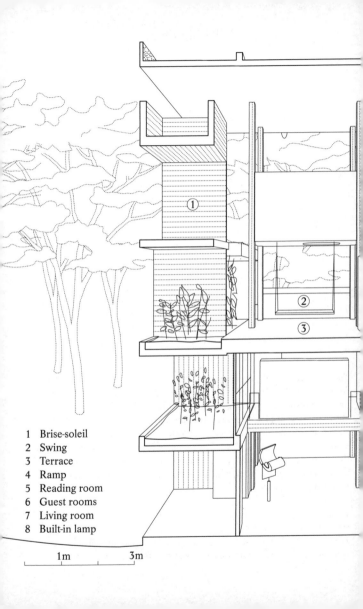

1 Brise-soleil
2 Swing
3 Terrace
4 Ramp
5 Reading room
6 Guest rooms
7 Living room
8 Built-in lamp

1m   3m

Villa Shodhan

Pushcarts

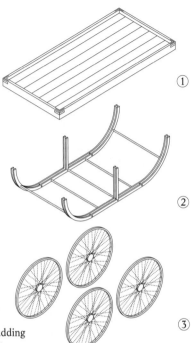

1 Timber cladding
2 Steel structure
3 Bicycle wheels

A basic pushcart is built out of bicycle wheels, timber and steel tubes. It is used all over India in a variety of ways. Pushcarts offer their owners great flexibility. The sheer numbers of vendors using pushcarts underline the relevance of this Indian phenomenon. On the streets, they form public micro-spaces for trading and communication. They are the physical support for the vendors' way of life. Here is a fine example of one item used in manifold ways.

Location: All over Ahmedabad, but usually on the main streets.
Hint: Gujari Bazaar (p. 84) is a good place to buy a pushcart.

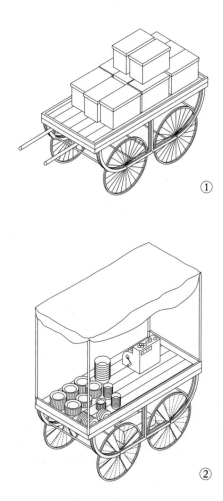

① ②

0,5m   1,5m

Pushcarts

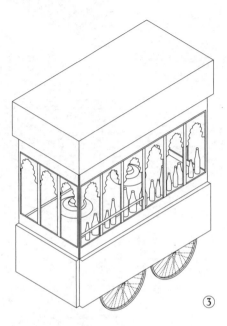

③

1 People use pushcarts for transportation of all kinds. By attaching
  pushing handles, even transporting passengers is possible.
2 Salesmen use the pushcart as a mobile selling unit. Often multiple
  pushcarts form a temporary street market. Goods range from fruits
  and household items to electronic products. A pushcart offers the
  opportunity to take the goods to the customers. Pushcarts are
  adapted to improve the presentation of a product or to fashion
  a temporary shelter at night.
3 Converting a cart into an ice cream parlor requires modification
  of the basic cart to include freezer facilities and advertising.
  Large signs advertise the ice-cream and the name of the parlor.
  Behind the pushcart is a shady place to sit, created by an awning
  stretched over branches.

Mill Owners' Association

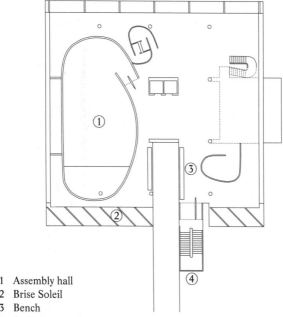

1 Assembly hall
2 Brise Soleil
3 Bench
4 Staircase

The structure is derived from the context: the building is oriented
according to the prevailing winds. It overlooks the river and the daily
spectacle of people washing clothes, buffaloes, and donkeys while
standing in the water. The east and west façades incorporate a deep
sun-screening structure, whereas the north and south façades have almost
no windows. The assembly hall is on the second floor, constructed of
thin, double-brick walls cladded with wood in a diagonal pattern.

Location: Near Ellis Bridge, opposite City Gold Cinema, Ashram Road
Architect: Le Corbusier, 1954
Program: Cotton Mill Owners' Headquarters

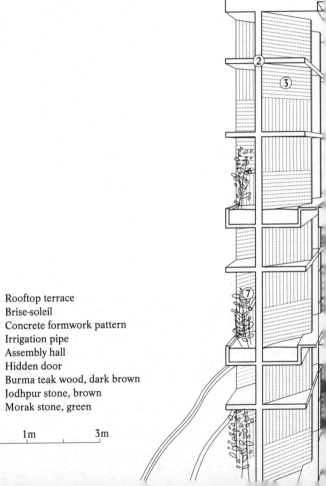

1 Rooftop terrace
2 Brise-soleil
3 Concrete formwork pattern
4 Irrigation pipe
5 Assembly hall
6 Hidden door
7 Burma teak wood, dark brown
8 Jodhpur stone, brown
9 Morak stone, green

1m   3m

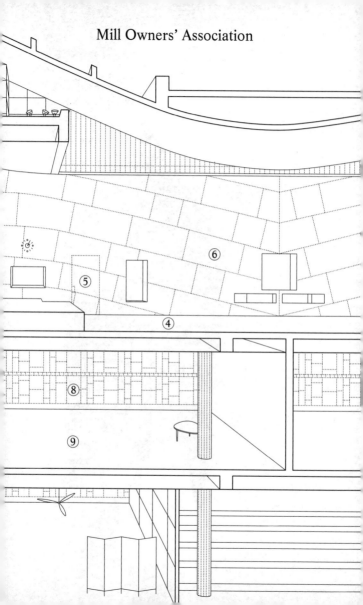

Mill Owners' Association

Navrangpura

The façade of the Navrangpura Bus Stop functions as a huge billboard.
The whole building has been totally covered over time by hand-painted
advertisements. Under the layers of paint is a building designed by the
architect Charles Correa. Nowadays the bus terminal is not only used to
wait for buses. The upper floor houses a private engineering company.
During the day, the south side of the ground floor is full of waiting
passengers. The north side is an informal motorcycle taxi stand. Next
to it, a group of homeless people have erected an informal shelter. They
have extended their living space by incorporating the benches and fences,
which is tolerated by the travelers.

Location: Manav Nadir Road, Navrangpura
Architect: Charles Correa, 1962-63
Program: Bus stop and engineering company office

1　Bus stop
2　Informal shelter
3　Engineering company office
4　Steel reinforcement for future extension
5　Billboard

0,5m　　　1,5m

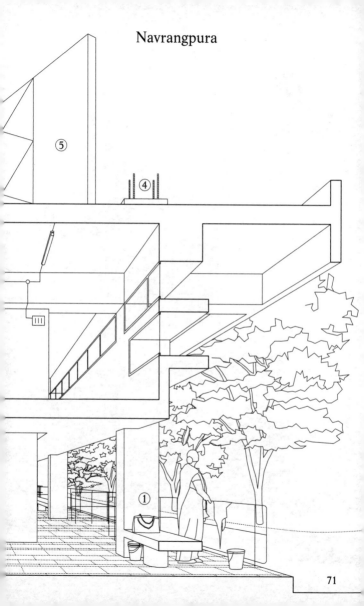

Gun House

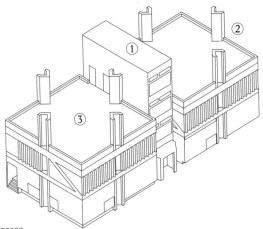

1 Staircase
2 Main structure
3 Free floor plan

The appearance of the Gun House has completely changed over time
as different tenants altered it to suit their own purposes. Initially it was
planned as an office building for the Ahmedabad Rifle Association. The
building consists of two separate blocks, each 12 m by 12 m. In between
the two blocks is a central section for air conditioning and toilet facilities.
The floor slab is a diagonal grid supported by four columns placed at
the mid points of each external wall, while are in turn strengthened by
diagonal braces to the corners. Thus an internal office space free from
obstructions is created. The Association still owns the ground floor. On
the upper floor there is a printing agency and a sweatshop. A repair shop
for motorcycles recently opened along the back façade.

Location: J P Chowk, Khanpur
Architect: Charles Correa, 1960-62
Program: Ahmedabad Rifle Association, motorcycle repair shop, printing
agency, sweatshop

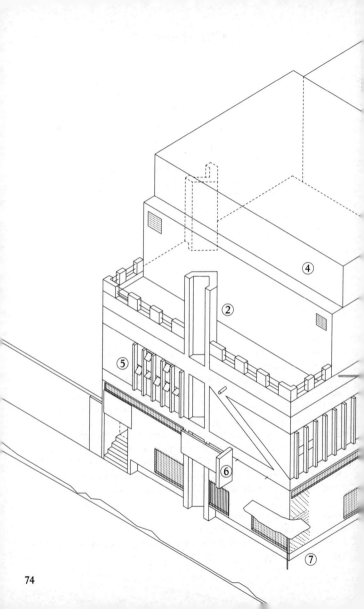

74

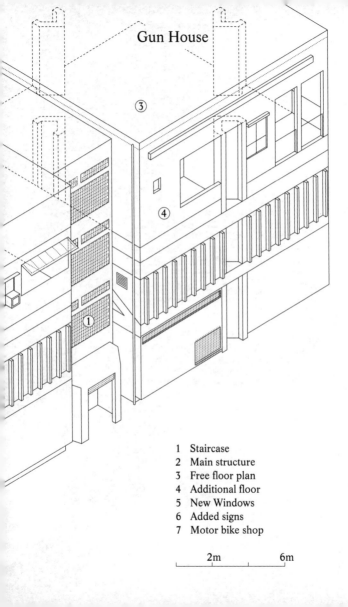

Gun House

1   Staircase
2   Main structure
3   Free floor plan
4   Additional floor
5   New Windows
6   Added signs
7   Motor bike shop

2m   6m

Central Bank

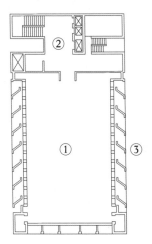

1 Office space
2 Elevators
3 Brise soleil façade

The Central Bank of India sits on the corner of one of the most important road junctions in Ahmedabad. You are bound to pass this iconic building sooner or later when exploring Ahmedabad from the back of a rickshaw. It is located between the east bank of the river, the New City, and the entrance to the Old City. The building sets itself apart from its surroundings with its massive concrete presence. On the ground floor there are customer services and ATM facilities. The next level houses a cafeteria. Above this are six more floors of offices, screened by concrete brise-soleil elements. This façade creates the urban identity of the tall building.

Location: Opposite Sidi Saiyad Mosque, Nehru Bridge Road
Architect: Balkrishna Doshi, 1967
Program: Regional Offices, 11,000 m²
Hint: Ask the guard to take you up to the roof terrace.

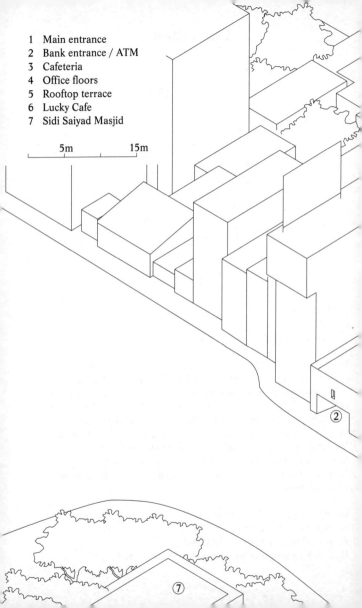

1 Main entrance
2 Bank entrance / ATM
3 Cafeteria
4 Office floors
5 Rooftop terrace
6 Lucky Cafe
7 Sidi Saiyad Masjid

5m   15m

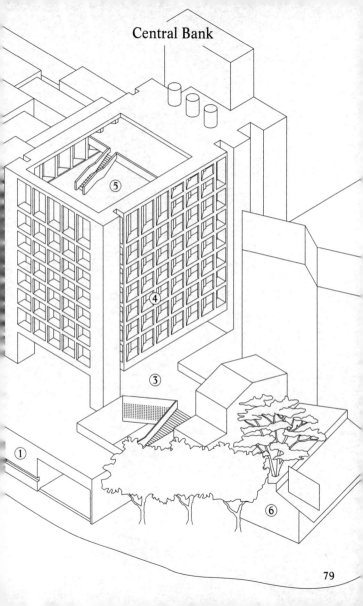

Central Bank

Lucky Cafe

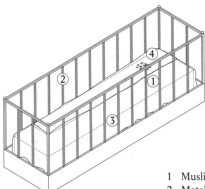

1 Muslim grave stone
2 Metal fence
3 Green blanket
4 Petals

To relish a satisfying cup of chai, Lucky Cafe is the place to go. This popular haunt, situated on a busy corner in the east end of town, is patronized mainly for its marsala chai. The charm of the place is in the mystery of the graves that are found nearby. Lucky Cafe originally started as a handcart under the shade of a neem tree, next to several graves. As business grew, so did the shop, eventually expanding around the graveyard and the tree. Though the owners do not know whose graves these are, they continue to offer incense, flowers, and respect as they have complete faith that these departed souls are behind Lucky's luck! One possible theory is that the graves belong to defeated enemy soldiers buried near the spot where they fell. This general area, known as Lal Darwaza, has witnessed several medieval battles. Lucky runs a family restaurant next door that serves food and juice in addition to the standard items.

Location: Lucky Cafe, opposite Sidi Sayyid ni Jali, near Dinbai Tower, Lal Darwaza
Open: 5 a.m. until midnight, daily
Chai: 20 Rupees

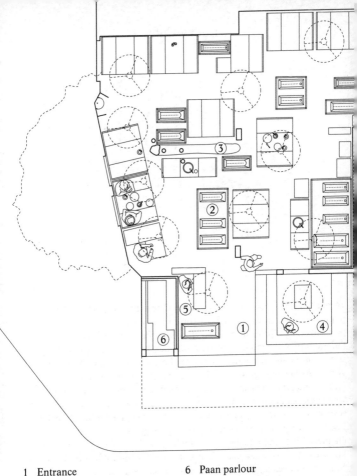

1 Entrance
2 Grave
3 Neem tree
4 Kitchen
5 Cashier

6 Paan parlour
7 Bicycle repair shop
8 Tomb
9 Mirzapur Road

1m   3m

Lucky Cafe

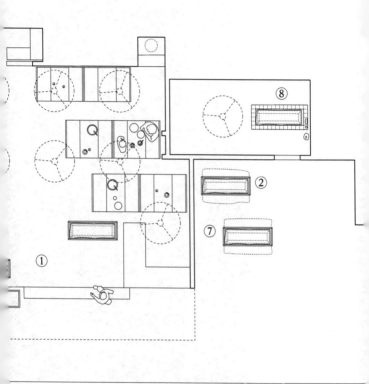

Gujari Bazaar

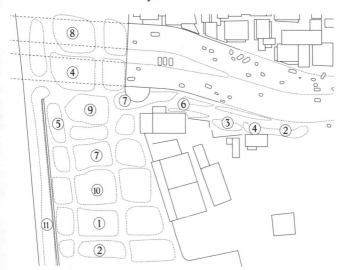

1 Clothing: pants, saris, shoes
2 Cookware: pots and pans
3 Food: traditional food, juices
4 Antiques: old watches
5 Knick knacks: postcards, jewelry, decorative accessories, vinyl records
6 Books
7 Furniture: beds, shelves, pushcarts
8 Living
9 Tools
10 Electronics
11 Animals: goats, chicken, sheep

Gujari Bazaar is the largest open air market in Ahmedabad. You can literally find everything here, from furniture, to shoes, to live animals. Each trader specializes in one product category. Many traders display their products on blankets. The market is divided into different product areas.

Location: Next to Ellis Bridge, along Sabarmati Riverfront Old City
Organizer: Ahmedabad Gujari Association, since 1415
Program: Trader-organized market, 500 m²
Hint: The market opens on Sundays at dawn.

1 Trader
2 Carpet
3 Pliers
4 Wrenches
5 Sandpaper
6 Customer

0,3m ⌞_____⌟ 1m

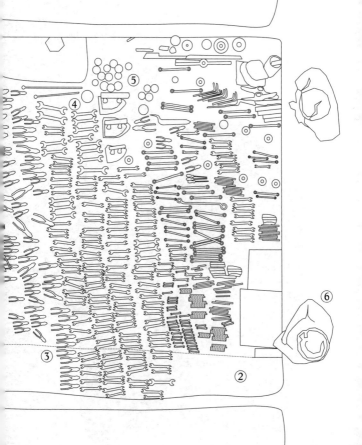

Premabhai Hall

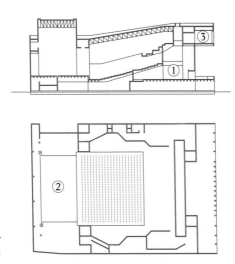

1 Foyer
2 Stage
3 Bar

The Premabhai hall is located in the Old City of Ahmedabad. Due to its
large dimension, the building is reminiscent of an ancient monumental
sculpture. Doshi designed this post-Corbusian Brutalist piece of
architecture in 1956 as a modern public theater. The wide stage (100 m)
provides perfect conditions for western ballet performances. The roof
has a generous sky terrace with a fantastic view of its vibrant historical
surroundings. As the theater was closed down in 1997, the building is
now an empty shell. Nevertheless, its sheer volume is still able to give
character to its architectural context, forming and structuring public
spaces. Premabhai Hall has now become a hollow guardian of the Old
City of Ahmedabad waiting to be woken from its long sleep.

Location: Opposite Bhadrakali Temple, Bhadra
Architect: Balkrishna Doshi, 1956-72
Program: Auditorium with 975 seats: cultural dance and music events,
conferences, meetings, and other types of gatherings

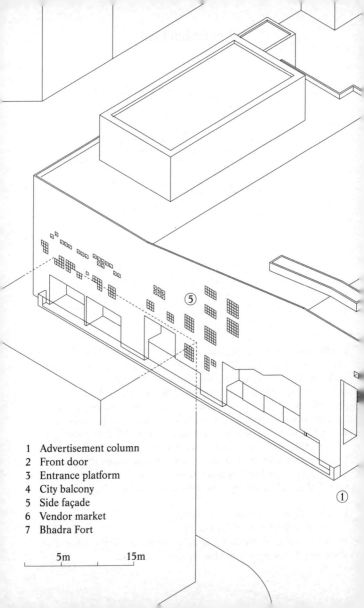

1 Advertisement column
2 Front door
3 Entrance platform
4 City balcony
5 Side façade
6 Vendor market
7 Bhadra Fort

⑤

①

5m   15m

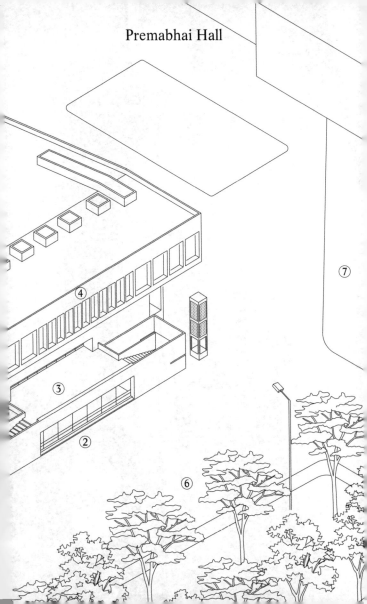

Premabhai Hall

Mahendi Rang Lagyo

Mahendi Rang Lagyo is a refreshment stand situated on the outer wall of a temple just beside a main street in the center of the old city. The shop sells freshly made fruit juices and lassis. About eighteen customers can be seated. Monobloc chairs face each other in rows like at a bus stop. Temple visitors can pass down the middle. On request the staff will also bring the tasty juices to a nearby seating area or to your motorcycle or rickshaw on the street.

Location: Mahendi Rang Lagyo Fruit Juice House, Relief Road, near Gheekanta Crossing
Dates from: The temple is 18th century, the shop was extended in the 1980s.

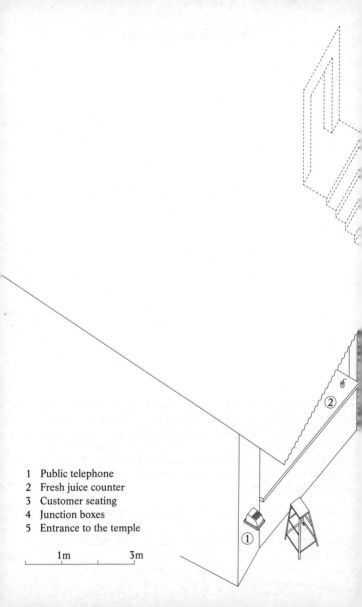

1 Public telephone
2 Fresh juice counter
3 Customer seating
4 Junction boxes
5 Entrance to the temple

1m   3m

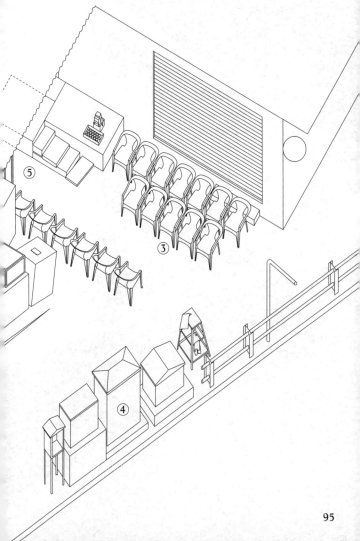

Chai Wallah

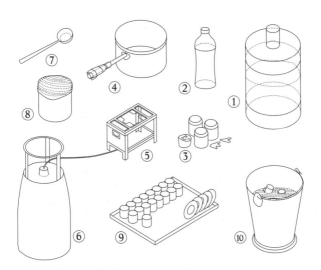

1 Water
2 Fresh milk
3 Tea and spices
4 Chai pot
5 Stove
6 Gas cylinder
7 Ladle
8 Filter
9 Cups
10 Cleaning bucket

A small passage along Relief Road, the entrance to a housing cluster, known and used by locals. A place to park a motorcycle or leave the rubbish. Just enough space for the chai wallah to open his small shop! He has placed a few metal boxes next to the concrete wall. On top of these are a stove, tea glasses, and ingredients. This is all he needs. Suddenly, this transitional alley has become a place to have a rest and a chat while sipping a hot chai. Inside the inner gate, the chai wallah has built himself a small improvised shelter.

Location: Old City, Relief Road, near the Post Office
Program: Chai wallah, apartment, entrance

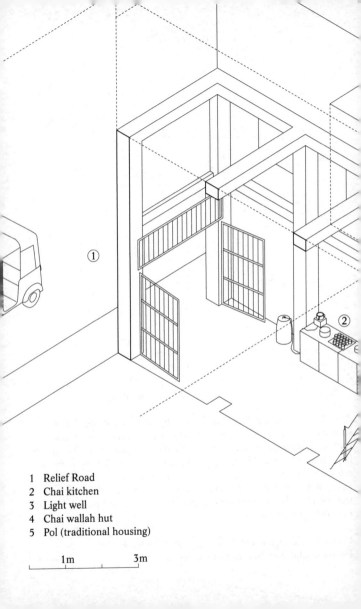

1 Relief Road
2 Chai kitchen
3 Light well
4 Chai wallah hut
5 Pol (traditional housing)

1m   3m

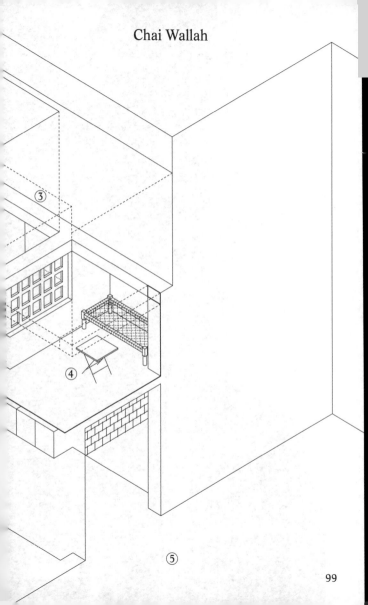

Jama Masjid

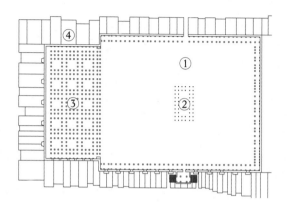

1 Jama Masjid Courtyard
2 Praying area
3 Wash basin
4 Shops

Visitors struggle to locate the entrance to the main mosque of
Ahmedabad – the Jama Masjid. It is probably the biggest open square
in the town and can only be entered in two places. It is easy to miss the
narrow openings between the shops. Over time, the outer wall of the
mosque has become completely colonized by small shops and houses.
The small balconies behind and above the shops belong to the outer
wall of the mosque. Passing through the entrance gate, you reach the
substantial inner courtyard.

Location: Jama Masjid Mosque, Jama Masjid Lane, extension of
Mahatma Gandhi Road, to the east of Teen Darwaja
Built in 1423 by Sultan Ahmed Shah
Size: 8,500 m²

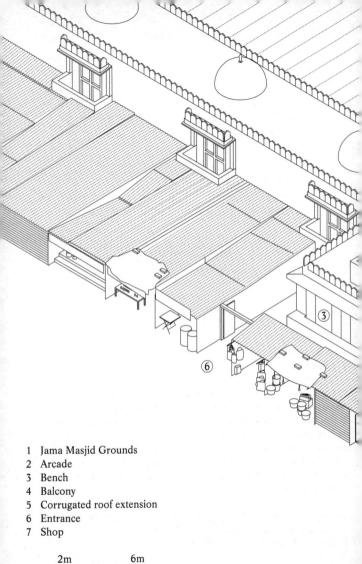

③

⑥

1 Jama Masjid Grounds
2 Arcade
3 Bench
4 Balcony
5 Corrugated roof extension
6 Entrance
7 Shop

|———|———|
2m   6m

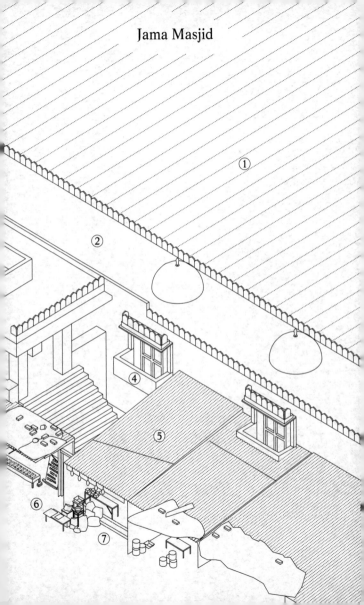

Jama Masjid

①

②

④

⑤

⑥

⑦

Manek Chowk

In the heart of the old city of Ahmedabad lies the small market square
Manek Chowk. It is crowded and lively and forms the beating heart
of the area. Old Havelis (private mansions with a courtyard) and Pols
(traditional gated communal housing) surround the square, which
is situated right between the ancient Kings and Queens Tombs.
Manek Chowk is used for different purposes at different hours of
the day and night:

5 a.m.: Farmers drive their cattle to sleepy Manek Chowk to feed them.
Feeding a cow on the morning of an important day brings good luck –
this is a Hindi proverb.

7 a.m.: Car parking now begins. When the cows have left, the first
vendors start to arrive and set up their stalls. The children treat it as a
playground before they start school.

4 p.m.: This is the most crowded time every day of the week – you may
want to avoid it! Stalls and shops selling all kinds of things, from clothes
to vegetables, can be found here.

8 p.m.: Every evening, the square turns into a huge food court with the
best street food in Ahmedabad. There is a great atmosphere as everyone
sits at large tables or on carpets on the ground.

Location: Old City, between the ancient Kings and Queens Tombs
Duration: 24 hours a day

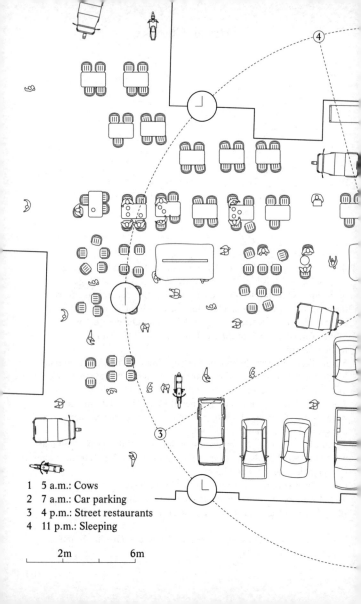

1 5 a.m.: Cows
2 7 a.m.: Car parking
3 4 p.m.: Street restaurants
4 11 p.m.: Sleeping

2m   6m

Manek Chowk

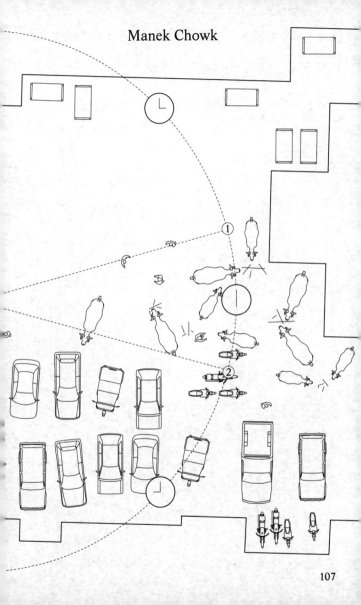

Paan Parlour

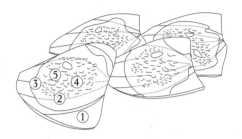

1 Betel leaf
2 Slaked lime paste
3 Areca nut
4 Chewing tobacco
5 Spices

Paan is a preparation of betel nut (sometimes also mixed with spices and/ or chewing tobacco), bound with slaked lime and rolled in a betel leaf. It also exists as a sweet version without tobacco. It is sold in small shops called paan parlors. Here men meet and buy products such as shaving gear, a variety of tobaccos, and drinks. These items are placed at the front of the shop and extend the actual shop space during opening hours. But most customers come for paan. Each portion is freshly prepared by the shopkeeper. A small crowd stands around the Paan parlor most of the day, chatting and chewing paan.

Location: East end of Manek Chowk, Old City
Program: Paan shop, meeting place

Paan Parlour

1 Market
2 Street temple
3 Shops
4 Paan parlor
5 Male customers
6 Red paan spit mark

a Paan
b Pillow to sit comfortably
c Soft drinks and water
d Snacks (hanging up)
e Additional storage in boxes
f Halogen light
g Loudspeaker

0,3m   1m

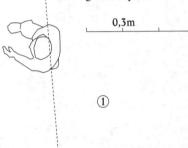

①

⑥

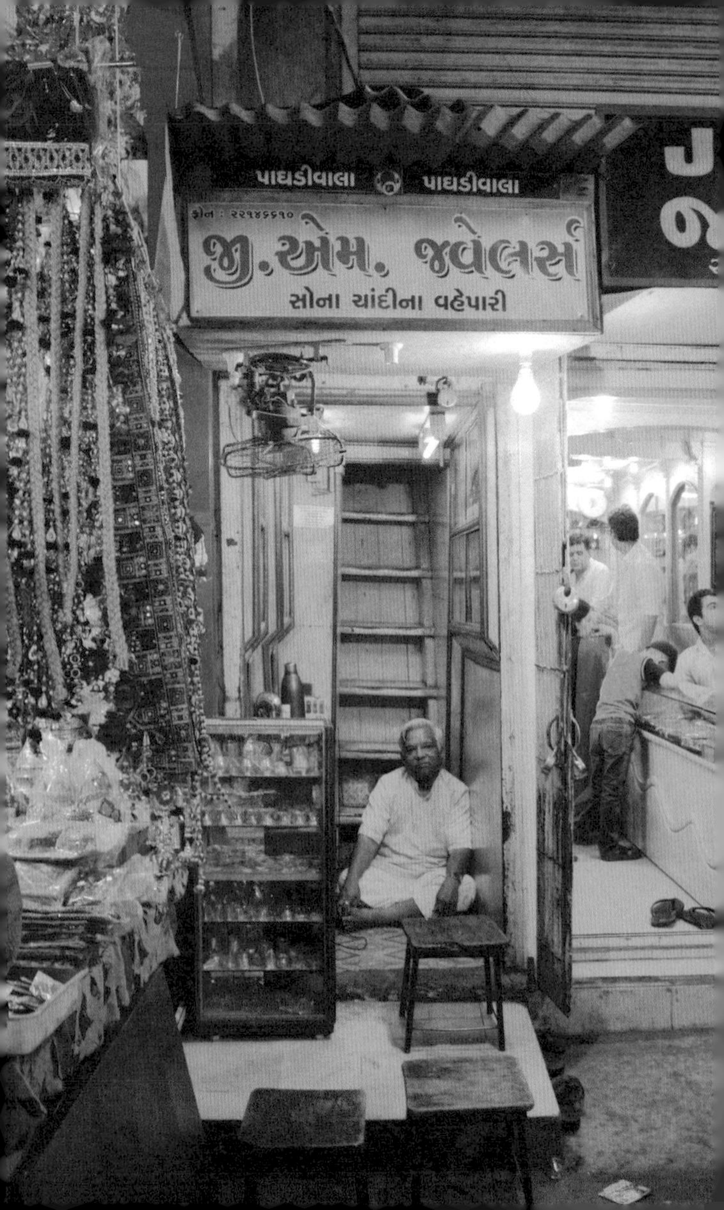
પાઘડીવાલા પાઘડીવાલા
ફોન : ૨૨૧૪૬૬૧૦
જી.એમ. જવેલર્સ
સોના ચાંદીના વહેપારી

Shree Ran Jeweler

Shops in Ahmedabad generally have a single owner. These micro-shops are optimized to the very last detail and typically extend onto the streets. Often they provide something as well as their main business. In old housing communities the function of the otla space (a raised transitional area between the street and house) was to communicate between the public and private realms. Now the micro-shop has taken over this function. Passers-by, friends, and customers are welcomed in to take a seat on one of the chairs for a chat. From the store the owner can access the upper floor, which is either rented out or used as a storage space. The private living spaces are on the second and third floor.

Location: Madan Gopal Haveli Marg, Old City
Program: Gold and silver salesman, entrance hall to the apartment

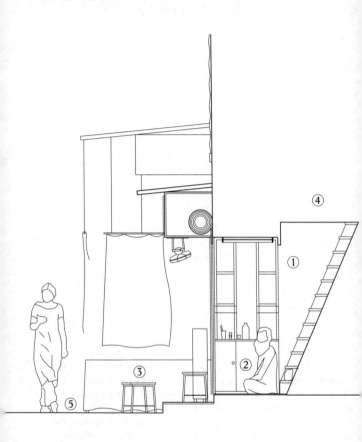

1 Shop
2 Showcase
3 Customer space
4 Living space
5 Street

0,5m   1,5m

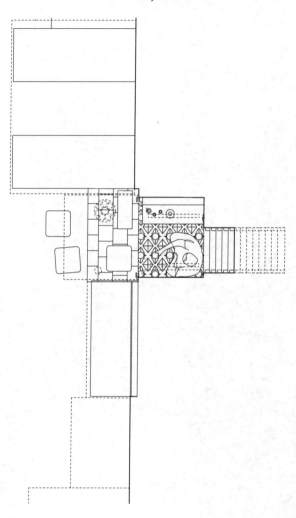

Outside Sleeping

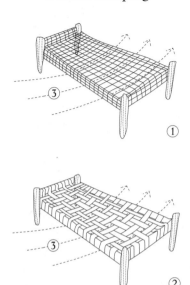

1 Charpai bed (Wooden frame bordering
   a set of knotted ropes)
2 Niwar bed (Wooden frame with woven
   niwar tape made of plastic or textile)
3 Breeze

Occupied outdoor space is very common on the streets of Ahmedabad.
Because of the heat, poor interior ventilation, and lack of space,
people shift their beds into the street. Locals even extend their living
space informally on top of buildings. The beds shown here are simple
constructions that maximize air circulation. In traditional Indian houses,
there was no particular room dedicated to sleeping. People just made
themselves comfortable wherever a suitable spot could be found. On
humid summer nights this was outside.

Location: On the streets of Ahmedabad, mostly in the old city

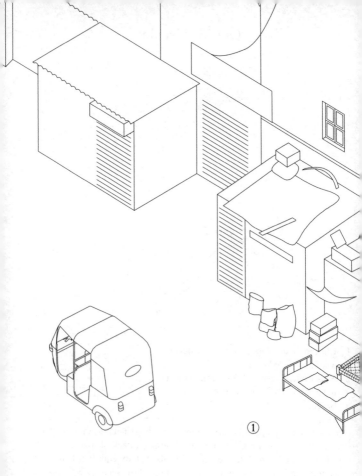

1 Street
2 Front door
3 Roof terrace
4 Charpai bed

|_____|_____|
        1m   3m

Public Praying

At the Ahmedabad Train Station a train arrives and there is a stop over of about ten minutes. Many travelers use the time to get a cool drink, a snack, or chai. New passengers are waiting to board the train. The public prayers happen quietly. When the train has stopped, without a word being said, an informal mosque is constructed of essential items. A basin with a tap, an area for removing shoes, a rug to kneel on (to guarantee cleanliness) and other items that border the temporary space. The street lamp acts as a "sutra," a ritual object protecting prayers from passers-by. An Imam sits in front of the group and leads the holy ritual. Within moments all this happens and then disappears again as everyone embarks to continue their journey.

Location: Ahmedabad Train Station, opposite Laxmi Bazaar, Saraspur
Duration: Ten minutes

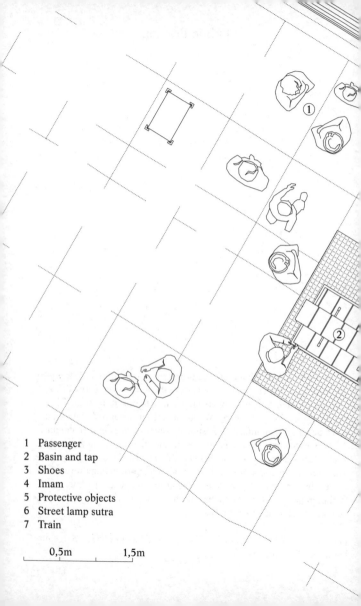

1 Passenger
2 Basin and tap
3 Shoes
4 Imam
5 Protective objects
6 Street lamp sutra
7 Train

0,5m   1,5m

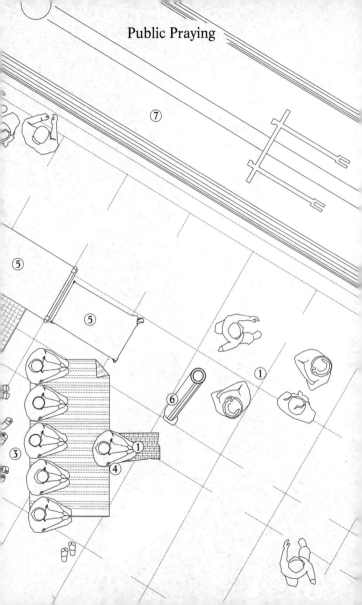

Public Praying

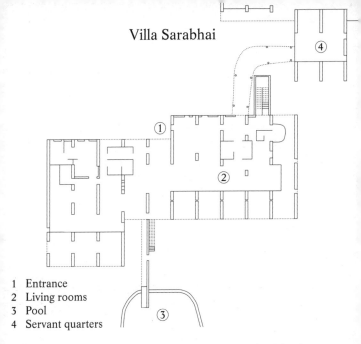

Villa Sarabhai

1 Entrance
2 Living rooms
3 Pool
4 Servant quarters

The Villa Sarabhai is situated in Shahibag on the east side of the river. Parallel brick walls create long rooms. Strong beams allow the creation of wide rooms and large windows. These spaces together form a long series of vaults. Lengthwise, the house extends into the garden. The veranda façade can be opened so that the house becomes a continuation of the garden. The flat rooftop is also accessible for leisure. Small trees, wild shrubs, and hanging plants cover the whole roof. The villa is owned by an art collector and houses a private collection of art objects. The armed housekeeper keeps unwanted visitors and monkeys at bay.

Location: Next to the Calico Textile Museum
Architect: Le Corbusier, 1951-55
Program: Residence of Mrs. Sarabhai
Hint: The housekeeper can be phoned via the House of MG or the Vastu Shilpa Foundation. It costs 500 Rupees per person for a restricted "tour" led by the staff.

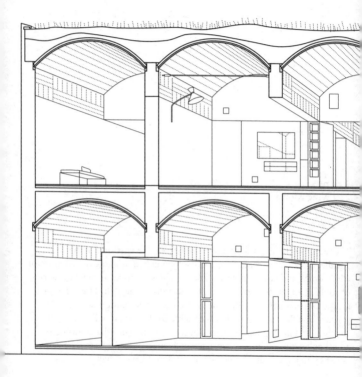

Villa Sarabhai

1 Roof garden
2 Concrete layer
3 Concrete beam in "béton brut" finishing
4 Catalonian brick vaults
5 Brick walls, painted
6 Brick walls, unfinished
7 Floor in black Madras stone
8 Ventilation element
9 Waterslide

1m   3m

Gandhi Ashram

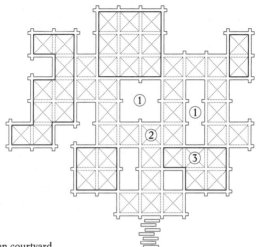

1 Open courtyard
2 Roofed circulation space
3 Enclosed exhibition space

The museum stands next to the house where Gandhi lived before he set out on the historic Salt March to Dandi. It exhibits letters, photographs, and other documents from the Freedom Movement. Thanks to its modular system, the structure of the museum is able to expand, in order to house the growing collection. The modules are either enclosed spaces, semi-enclosed spaces, or spaces simply left open as courtyards. Visitors move freely between them. The museum is constructed of brick walls, stone floors, wooden doors, tiled roofs, and concrete channels that act as beams and gutters. Light and ventilation are provided by adjustable wooden louvers that make glass unnecessary.

Location: Sarbarmati River Bank, Ashram Road, Old Vadaj
Architect: Charles Correa, 1958-63
Program: Memorial Museum, 2,300 m²

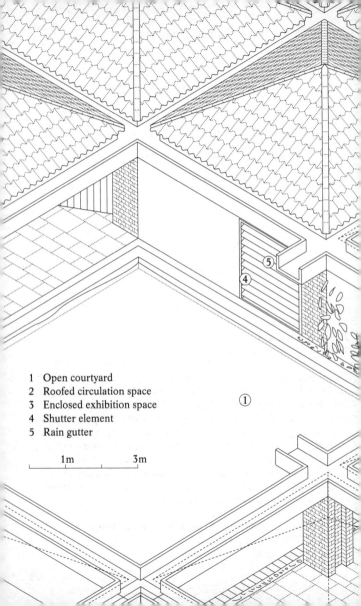

1 Open courtyard
2 Roofed circulation space
3 Enclosed exhibition space
4 Shutter element
5 Rain gutter

1m   3m

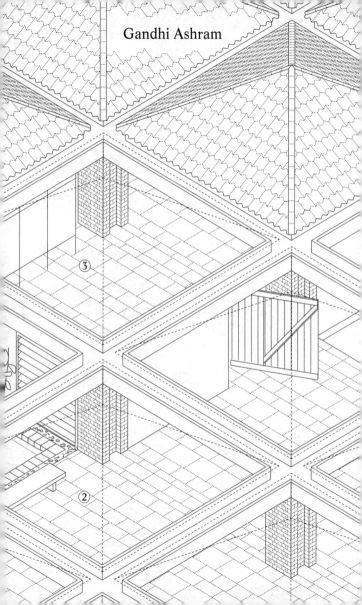

Gandhi Ashram

③

②

Curtain Loggia

The design of the Sola Housing Estate allows for wider and more spacious streets than is customary in India. A lot of the new houses have spacious loggias. Residents hang large, soft green curtains around the loggias. This shades the loggia spaces from the sun and provides privacy. This in-between space creates an extended living area that is equipped with laundry lines, charpoys (Indian beds), and other furniture. Fans cool the air. Sometimes a relaxing swing is set up. It seems to have become customary to hang a green curtain in front of your loggia in the Sola area.

Location: Sola Housing, Sola
Hint: Walk around the area to see more houses with green-curtained loggias.

1 Curtain
2 Railing
3 Swing
4 Fan
5 Laundry line
6 Window

1m   3m

Curtain Loggia

Publisher's Afterword

There are many ways to discover a city as a traveller. You can follow the footsteps of a tourist guide taking you on a scenic tour of a city's most famous sights. Or you might use an architecture guide listing all the fancy buildings you have to see and check them off one by one. Both ways of seeing thrive on the logic of the "must-see" spectacle, a notion which could give you the impression that discovering cities is some kind of work.

We almost never use guidebooks when we are about to experience a new city. We much more enjoy getting to know it through the eyes of friends who live there. They take you on a dérive of places that matter to them, to their everyday lives and their personal experience of their city. And as you discover the city on their heels, passing by strangely fascinating buildings, an effervescent night market here and a hidden courtyard there, you feel how the layers of touristic conditioning start to unpeel from your mind. Surreptitiously you settle into the much more exciting identity of a temporary local. You begin to see the world around you as an environment in which you might potentially live, and not as yet another "exotic" location that you quickly consume before hopping to the next one. If there is exoticism involved at all, then it lies in the everyday, the ordinary, the zillions of minute wonders that you experience as you allow the place to absorb you mentally and physically.

But sometimes you don't have a friend to show you around in a city that is foreign to you. We wondered whether a book could give you a similarly captivating and personal introduction and, if so, how exactly the book would need to be different from regular architectural guides. One of the issues that bothers us most about the latter is their tendency to represent the city as a collection of its most striking buildings. This is a troublesome misconception in at least two ways. First, it ignores the fact that cities are for the most part made of rather unspectacular buildings—which are nonetheless important because they build the fabric that defines a city. If the buildings we normally find in books are the cherries, then those other, inconspicuous buildings are the cake. A city made exclusively of architectural cherries would be a bizarre nightmare, a cacophony of spectacles that ultimately drown each other out. We clearly need the generic to alternate with the specific in order to appreciate a city, and therefore we think an architectural guide to a city should not simply be a beauty contest—it needs to embrace the seemingly unspectacular as well. Second, and maybe even more importantly, the cherry-only architectural guidebook almost invariably fails to acknowledge that cities don't consist of buildings alone, but also of the urban spaces shaped by buildings. It is the particular relationship of solid and void, of built and unbuilt space, that gives a city its characteristic profile. And although it's the urban space that we mostly inhabit when we discover a city, this magic public living room that gives a collective shelter to all its inhabitants and visitors is almost never given its due credit in conventional architectural guides.

This is exactly what we would like to overcome in this new series of "Architecture Reading Aids," of which this edition on Ahmedabad is the first installment. The book celebrates the urban space of Ahmedabad in both its solid and void materialities. It introduces you to a selection of fantastic buildings built by famous architects such as Le Corbusier, Louis Kahn, Charles Correa, and Balkrishna

Publisher's Afterword

Doshi. Their buildings are what draw most architectural visitors to Ahmedabad. But the book also treats its readers to a puzzling variety of idiosyncratic public spaces that you normally don't find in books, but which are absolutely essential for an understanding of Ahmedabad's unique urban phenomenology.

These are spontaneous appropriations of space: a café arranged underneath a piece of cloth stretched out for shade, a little shop nestled in the poché of a wall with the merchant fitting in perfectly, or beds placed on the street that people push out of their sticky houses to sleep better in the nocturnal breeze. It is a kind of performative micro-urbanism of the people, who realize their personal demands very directly by building small spatial installations in public space. We find these appropriations touching and ingenious in the way they create a lot of spatial use value for daily life with minimum means. We wish public space in European cities were as useful and inventive as in Ahmedabad, and we found that we could learn a lot from it.

Even though these examples are not buildings and were very likely not designed by architects, they are documented in exactly the same way as the buildings by the famous architects mentioned above. For the experience of the city, they are just as important as the latter, especially so in a city like Ahmedabad. Hence the authors of the book have drawn these performative city spaces as meticulously as the buildings, and described the functional scenarios of these vernacular urban moments as lovingly as those of the built masterpieces by Le Corbusier and his peers. The book makes no hierarchical distinction between architecture and the city. Both provide vital spaces for our lives.

The drawings are perhaps what most distinguishes this book from ordinary architectural guides, which generally rely on photographs. Our "Architecture Reading Aid" of course also features photographs of the projects. They communicate the atmosphere of the places and will help readers recognize them on their way through the city. But the illustrations arguably add another, deeper dimension. The axonometric drawings allow readers to understand how a situation is actually spatially configured. By omitting color and textures and focusing exclusively on black lines on white ground, the drawings emphasize the parts of these buildings and places that are most crucial for understanding how they work, giving you a lot of information you could not get from a photograph.

Lastly, a word about the selection of examples. This selection is not meant to be representative of the whole city. It presents the subjective view of the authors, who lived there for several weeks and decided to document some of the places they grew fond of. The book invites readers to follow in the footsteps of the authors—like the friends we always love to have show us their city. They can learn to see the city first through the authors' eyes, then develop their own vision, this time based on their own preferences, interests, and desires. In this way the book might help its readers to break free of the scripted view of the tourist and instead adopt the perspective of a temporary local, someone who engages with the city in a visceral way rather than just consuming it visually. That's what the book did for us, at least, and for this we would like to express our most heartfelt gratitude to its authors.

– Ilka & Andreas Ruby